JESUS OUR LEADER

A GUIDE TO THE THOUGHT OF
KARL HEIM

Jesus
Our Leader

by

E. L. ALLEN

London
HODDER & STOUGHTON

MADE AND PRINTED IN GREAT BRITAIN FOR HODDER AND STOUGHTON LIMITED, LONDON, BY C. TINLING AND CO., LTD., LIVERPOOL, LONDON AND PRESCOT.

CONTENTS

BIOGRAPHICAL NOTE . . . 6

1 THE TWO WORLD-VIEWS . . . 7

2 GOD 17

3 THE GROUND OF CERTAINTY . . 23

4 JESUS AS LORD 31

5 CONSUMMATION 39

KARL HEIM was born January 20, 1874, at Frauenzimmer in Württemberg. He studied theology at Tübingen and on graduation served for a time as pastor and teacher in Württemberg. He was Secretary to the German S.C.M. 1899-1902. His academic career began at Halle in 1907; he became Professor of Systematic Theology at Münster in 1914 and at Tübingen in 1902. He was in the forefront of the opposition to the German Faith Movement, one of whose leaders was a colleague at Tübingen, and which advocated the abandonment of Christianity for a ' new paganism ' with its roots in Germany's past. At present (1948) Heim is at work on a book dealing with the relation between religion and science.

THE TWO WORLD-VIEWS

IN his autobiography, Dr. L. P. Jacks tells of an old soldier who was looking, in a picture-gallery, at a painting by Lady Butler of a battle in which he had himself taken part. When he had surveyed it all over, he shook his head, and remarked: 'But it wasn't at all like that when you were in it.' There we have brought before us a distinction on which Heim is never weary of insisting. There are two views of an event, one showing how it appears from the outside and the other what it is to one who actually participates in it. The spectator and the actor will give two quite different accounts of the same occurrence. The bored invigilator, struggling to keep awake on a hot summer afternoon, has virtually nothing in common with the harassed, over-worked student, whose only chance of a university education lies in success in this ordeal. Yet they are within the same four walls, and it is the same examination which brings them together !

Generalising, we may say that there are two world-views, one objective and scientific, one subjective and personal, one static and the other dynamic. The static world-view is the one with which common-sense operates, and on it has been built that account of the world which most people still regard as ' scientific.' For it there is a number of objects, which fall into the two groups of ' things ' and ' persons,' and each object occupies its own particular portion of space. The relations which obtain between these objects are causal, so that when anything takes place we look for somewhere in its neighbourhood if possible, in which something else had previously taken place of which it can be considered the effect. The world is a vast causal system in which we are ourselves embedded, our knowledge being the effect of the operation upon our minds of objects external to us. We may cherish the illusion of freedom but, on this assumption, we are in fact part of a causal nexus, our actions at any given moment being simply the result of the particular combination of circumstances at the preceding moment. The triumph of this explanation in terms of cause and effect is Laplace's suggestion that, given the knowledge by an all-comprehending intelligence of the exact condition of things throughout the world at this moment, it should be possible for such an intelligence to deduce therefrom all the details of the past and all the complexities of the future.

What place is left for religion in this world-mechanism? None whatever. It is only ' a cry for help thrown out at some forlorn point in the world's immeasurable night, in the midst of an infinitude containing only rolling masses of matter, a cry which rends the air for a moment within an insignificant radius about its place of origin, to be swallowed up next moment in the icy silence of world-space and lost.'*

What have we to oppose to this grim prospect? Primarily, the fact that in our immediate experience there is something which does not fit into the causal scheme at all.

* *God Transcendent*, 174.

That scheme is the work of human minds, and those minds must have been able to stand outside the causal sequence and take note of it. The world of objects exists for *me* as *my* object, and there must be something in me therefore which can never be reduced to an object. My self is not just one more thing to be observed and accounted for, simply because there must be that which can observe and give account. An object presupposes a subject which, *ipso facto*, is not an object. True, I can become an object to myself in self-knowledge, but the self which knows lies in a region beyond anything which can be objectified. When I repent of my past, I distinguish the whole of my past life as the object which I survey from that in me which reviews, disowns, and seeks to be free from, it.

The very existence of that world of objects with which common sense and Newtonian physics work therefore involves another order of reality, one which is non-objectifiable. This belongs to the inner side of our experience as the other to the outer side. Can we define more closely the nature of the

non-objectifiable ? If it is inaccessible to
scientific investigation, there is for all that
nothing strange or far-fetched about it. It
is indeed more real than anything else, for
in it we live and move and have our being.
This self which is always *knower* and never
that which is known, is at the same time
will. In willing and action we have the
assurance that there is a realm of freedom
and not merely a causal chain. Nothing
can convince me that my action is unreal ;
the determinist even acts as though we were
free when he tries to convince me that I
am not ! Again, his explanations only cover
what has already taken place, whereas freedom lives in the thrilling and hazardous
moment in which the future has still to
be made. Hence the world-view which immediate experience authenticates is dynamic
through and through. Nor can the category
of volition be confined to the human sphere.
In the actual moment in which one experiences a natural catastrophe, as when one's
house reels beneath the onslaught of a ty-
phoon, even civilised man reverts for the
time being to the mentality of primitive

peoples and feels himself engaged in a struggle against some hostile will. Only afterwards, when the storm has ceased, does he fit it neatly into the causal pattern.

Only afterwards—yes, we can see now how, given the dynamic world-view, the static arises out of it. It is the transition from present to past which effects the transformation. For we are spectators of the past, whereas we are actors in the present. Reality is known directly in living experience alone : it is only described, perhaps it is caricatured, when it is got at second-hand by observation of what has gone by. ' The objective world, with the spatial order in which it is spread out before us, is like the set metal shape which emerges in a cooled state from the red-hot furnace.'* A simple illustration of what happens in consequence of such a change of standpoint is furnished by the procedure of a tennis-coach. After he has served a ball himself, he will split up the single action into half a dozen for the benefit of the novice, showing him how he places his feet, grasps the racket, throws

* *Ibid.*, 188.

the ball, and so on. He has substituted a series of states for a total movement, because he has substituted a bit of reality as observed for a corresponding bit of reality as lived through. The account which the tennis-coach gives of his service is for certain purposes a necessary one, but who would say that it is as faithful to the facts as the sense of mastery with which he simply throws the ball into the air and brings the racket down upon it with a swift, sure stroke that sends it flashing across the net?

We have thus a whole series of equivalent distinctions, between the static and the dynamic, the objectifiable and the non-objectifiable, the past and the present. Closely parallel to this is a further distinction of which Heim makes great use, though it is neither original with him nor peculiar to him. It is the distinction between the I-It relation and the I-Thou relation. The classic discussion of this, of course, is in Martin Buber's richly profound book *Ich und Du*, of which an English version is happily available.*

* *I and Thou*, tr. Ronald Gregor Smith.

The I-It relation obtains between the self and its objects, the I-Thou relation between the self and other selves. To put it in this way, however, is to overlook the all-important fact that the self which knows objects is not the same as the self which knows other persons. In the first case, I reduce myself to an impersonal intelligence common to all who have reached a particular stage of mental development. I may indeed go so far in the process of depersonalisation as to eliminate myself entirely and substitute a camera for the actual registration of an object ! In the second case, it is as a total personality that I attach myself to another. I may not manipulate him as I would a thing, I must respect his individuality and independence. That is what makes the casual contacts and the conventionalised intercourse of modern society so unsatisfactory ; we feel that we are employing only part of our selves, that we are touching others at a point on the surface, not encountering them in giving and receiving at the deeper level of genuine selfhood. The I-Thou relation admits, to be sure, of gradations, being not the same with children as with adults, but there is something of it even in our dealing with domestic animals. Again, life requires both relations, we pass continually from one to the other. What is of supreme importance is that we should resist the temptation, to which we are always exposed, to degrade our encounter with persons to the mere observation and handling of things.

Two sentences from Buber will show Heim's debt to him : " So long as the heaven of Thou is spread out over me, the winds of causality cower at my heels, and the whirlpool of fate stays its course." "True beings are lived in the present, the life of objects is in the past."* There is an order of reality here which science cannot master but which it has no right to deny.*

Indeed, as Heim points out, science is no longer itself satisfied with the classical physics which ruled the Western mind since Newton's day. The scientist speaks no longer of things or of matter, but of energy-quanta, waves, and fields of force. He may even

* *I and Thou*, 9, 13.

suggest that the waves he speaks of represent degrees of probability in our knowledge rather than anything in the external world. But the distinction between the static and the dynamic world-views rests on philosophical grounds and is independent of changes in the language of science.

2

GOD

ONE point, for example, which is of immense importance and is not affected by any scientific developments, is the element of brute fact in the world. Even if we could suppose that everything which has taken place or will ever take place was involved necessarily in the original distribution of matter from which our world evolved, we are still left with that original distribution as something which must simply be accepted and cannot be explained. We think of time as a homogeneous medium in which objects are planted out, as it were, and no one point in space is distinguished in any way from another. Yet there is one such point which for me is 'here,' and which as such is central, with everything else in space arranged around it. I can give no reason why that particular point

should be singled out thus. So with the
'now,' the instant of time from which I
reckon all others as either past or present.
So with my selfhood, that modification of
consciousness which is unique, which is the
pivot on which my whole experience turns.
These things just are so. They are Destiny.

At this point we are confronted by the
supreme question of human life and one
which each has to answer for himself. How
shall I think of this Destiny? There are two
possibilities open: I may see in it either
chance or God. Either it is something which
just happens to be or there is in it a purpose
which aims at my good. In the first case,
I shall either capitulate to the circumstances
of my life or rebel against them; in the
second, I shall accept them as the expression
of highest wisdom and seek to cooperate
with its intention in them. The choice between these two alternatives is less something we make than something which is
made for us. There are those for whom
'the accent of eternity' has fallen on some
particular task, whose consciences have been
laid under constraint by an ethical impera-

tive, who know themselves called to play a man's part in this problematical world. For such, God *is* and they respond to him with their whole being. In the language of the previous section, he is to be found by the actor and not by the spectator, within the dynamic world-view, not the static, in an I-Thou, not an I-It relation.

But while we cannot prove God, we can show how vain it is to seek him within the limits of the static world view, though that is precisely what men have again and again insisted on doing. We may illustrate this from a consideration of two ultimate questions.

Take first that of the *origin of things*. Here only two possibilities are open to us, as long as we remain within the limits of the world of objects in causal relations. We may take some point as the beginning and everything else as following from it : or we may take the world-process as a whole as the explanation of its parts. In the first place, what we are pleased to term the First Cause is obviously just one element in our known world which is promoted to the dignity of being prior to the rest and giving them, as it were, an initial push. It may be the cosmic egg of a primitive people or a certain distribution of matter for a modern scientist : in either case it is what religion speaks of as an idol, a bit of this world that is passed off as God. On the second hypothesis, we have in fact pantheism. As long as we operate with the static world-view, we are shut up to either idolatry or pantheism. We can get no farther.

Or take the second question, that of an *ultimate moral standard*. What ' ought ' we to do ? Clearly that is something quite different from a consideration of what brings pleasure, or what society approves, or even what the experience of the race has shown to be conducive to life. We demand to come under an authority, to have a mandate given to us from beyond ourselves. But where is such an authority to be found ? There are only the same two possibilities. We may take something or someone in this world and give ourselves over to that. It may be a leader or a class or a party or a nation ; whatever it is, it is an idol. Or we can accept ourselves as part of a great whole and take our standards from it. We do this when we define the good as what makes for human progress or what helps on the evolution of the race. But what are we then but pantheists?

We may be satisfied for a time with such answers, but sooner or later they will reveal themselves as inadequate. We shall find that within the limits of the static world-view there is no answer to the questions which torment us. God is not to be found there. We must therefore either abandon our quest and surrender ourselves to despair or venture on something altogether new. As was said above, we must seek God with our total selves in the realm of ethical decision and personal commitment.

What happens when we do this? It is not so much that we find God as that he comes to meet us. He comes to meet us bearing two names which before were incomprehensible, but which are now fraught with meaning. God is the Creator and the Lord. These two names declare that he answers the questions to which we could find no answer.

As the Creator, he is neither one element in the world nor the world itself seen as a whole : he is its origin and its goal, beyond it yet present at every point within it. As the Lord, he does not compete with other claimants for our allegiance, nor does he take us up into some mystical totality : he is the will which lays claim to the obedience of our wills. At the same time, he is the source of all authority which is exercised in this world and therefore also the judge of such authority. Finally, we must put the two titles together and say of God that he is at once Creator and Lord. He is at once, that is, the fountain-head from which we derive our being and the ultimate basis of all responsible action. By his will we are in this world and to him at the last we must render an account of the life which is his gift.

But let us not forget that this God is to be found, not by intellect but by faith, by the total devotion of the self.

3

THE GROUND OF CERTAINTY

THE problem which lies behind all with which we have been concerned so far is that of certainty. How can we know when we are in possession of the truth ? Normally we distinguish between two different kinds of truth. There are truths of reason and truths of fact. The first kind are based on the principle of contradiction : we accept them because it can be shown that to deny them would involve us in self-contradiction. These give absolute certainty but they are purely hypothetical. They only tell us, that is, that under certain conditions, certain results are to be looked for : whether those conditions ever do actually take place is something with which they are not in the least concerned. Truths of fact, on the other hand, are certain just in so far as they are immediate experiences. But since immediate experience is something only accessible to us in the earliest moments of conscious life, while everything which is not thus experienced by us is to some extent interpreted and coloured by what went before, it follows that all assertions about facts are tainted with some degree of uncertainty.

For religion, however, especially if, with the Lutheran, we think in terms of the soul's assurance of a gracious God and his eternal salvation, it is clear that something more is wanted. Neither timeless principles nor facts that are more or less probable can speak peace to an aroused and tormented conscience. In this realm, only an absolute assurance will suffice. But is it obtainable?

We can find the answer to that question if we first aggravate the problem beyond anything said hitherto. It is in the nature of that static world-view with which we normally operate that everything in it is relative and conditioned. I look out upon the world from my particular situation and you from yours, and it is not possible for us to exchange our points of view. When you describe the beauties of the countryside through which you passed in a bus, I remark with regret that I saw nothing, as I was standing up. When next we make the journey, conditions are the same for both. But our reports diverge widely, since I was interested in the villages through which we passed, you in the harvesters and their crop. Send a Communist and a Catholic to Russia to see the same things, and when they come back, it will seem as though they have been to different countries ! My philosophy of life is one natural to an Englishman of the twentieth century ; it would be sheer nonsense to a Japanese or to a Latin American, or even to my great-grandfather. So with moral standards. It is an offence to run a black market in peace, but a patriotic action in the same country when it is in enemy hands. The Christian ethic wins my consent : had I been born in China, the Confucian or the Buddhist ethic would have received my allegiance just as unquestionably. We might go on thus indefinitely. Everything belongs to a particular point in space and a particular moment in time. Everything is therefore relative and nothing is absolute.

If now we were asked to formulate the impossible, that which, the world being what it is, simply cannot be, we might say that it would be for one particular occurrence in space and time to possess absolute value, to be authoritative for all spaces and all times. Yet, if we are not to be wholly lost, this which cannot ever be is precisely what somehow *must* be. Our souls cry out for it as the only support which would bear us up in this shifting, ever-changing scene. Our doubts cannot be resolved till we lay hold on that which abides while all else passes. And we must be able actually to ' lay hold ' on it. No mere idea will suffice, for ideas pitted against brute facts will always be worsted. The absolute must become brute fact, a particular and perceptible event in this world, or there is no hope for us.

Here is something we desperately need, but something, it is clear, we cannot ourselves produce to meet our need. The absolute must come to us freely and in its own majesty, if it comes at all. The most that we can do is to show, in accordance with the argument up to this point, that

the static world-view does not exhaust reality,
so that what is impossible in terms of it
may still for all that be possible otherwise.
What we need is a fact. Then we open
the pages of the New Testament and read
of a man—but no ! there is more to it than
that. We actually meet there with a man
who claims to exercise the authority of God
in this world of space and time. He does
what only God can do, forgives sin and grips
the conscience with absolute moral authority.
He does not give advice, he commands.
' Ye have heard,' he says, ' that it was said
unto them of old time, but I say unto you.'
Who is this man ? He is a carpenter of
Nazareth, his parents were known in the
village, and his death was no doubt entered
up in the records of the Roman court which
tried him. His disciples wrote of him as one
whom their eyes had seen and their hands
handled, and yet at the same time they con-
fessed in him the way, the truth and the life.
Across the centuries he speaks to us, bidding
us take up the cross and follow him.

What is it that makes us acknowledge
him as the one who brings God himself

to us? It is not that we have examined his credentials and decided that on the whole his claims are trustworthy. To examine his credentials is only possible if we have first decided to reject him as what he comes to be, our Lord. The only attitude open to us is one of decision, whether for him or against him. Nor is it that he lays upon us some sort of constraint. Rather does he free us from all constraints. To come to Jesus is at the same time to come into possession of ourselves. Half-men before, we are henceforth whole men. It is not merely that he satisfies our deepest spiritual needs. He does that, but we must add that we should never have known what those needs are had he not revealed them to us. He throws clear light on the mysteries of our existence. He does not give us a set of commands, but offers himself as our guide in all the changing circumstances of life. He rules us by the impression he makes upon our consciences, by convincing us that he is adequate as no other is. We do not think of him as superior to rival leaders, political or otherwise ; we feel that he stands alone and that any comparison would be an insult. For God himself comes to us in him. And the final, the most deeply felt conviction of faith is that he has dealt effectively with the sin which comes between us and God. ' God was in Christ, reconciling the world to himself.'

But is not all this imperilled by the fact that Jesus is a figure in ancient history, that we know of him only at second-hand and through documents which are open to criticism? Heim would answer that the witness of the disciples is authenticated in us when we believe. The Christ of whom they speak is no figure of the past, he is the living Lord whom we ourselves have met. We are therefore inwardly persuaded of the fidelity of their record in its main features. But that does not mean that the record in question is to be withdrawn to a sacred sphere which enquiry is forbidden to enter. All the methods of investigation which are available to us can and should be employed on the New Testament : our certainty of Christ is such that we can welcome every test as one which will vindicate him still more in the end.   The Christian must approach Christ in both ways, through personal devotion and through the historical study of the Gospels, and where these appear to clash he should accept the tension and live through it in faith.   Criticism cannot touch the certainties of faith, but faith has no right, and it has no need, to forbid criticism to enter its sanctuary.

4

JESUS AS LORD

THE starting-point of the Christian life is thus the acceptance of Jesus as Lord and of his claim upon us as absolute. We to-day should be better able to understand what this means than the pre-1914 generations could. For in those days men could live by general ideas, such as those which the French Revolution disseminated throughout Europe with its armies. But the shaken world which emerged from the war put its trust instead in persons, a Mussolini in Italy and a Gandhi in India. Men wanted someone to whom they could bind themselves in utter devotion and under whose guidance they could venture into the unknown future and master it. But these men can never satisfy the craving for a leader. Jesus alone can do that.

His leadership can only win us as we face

without evasion the realities of our human situation. We live, as we have seen, in a world of relativities, each of us bound to his particular moment in time and point in space. A score of possible courses of action present themselves to us and we waver in indecision between them : sometimes, to be sure, conscience speaks to us in imperative tones and for a moment we are lifted out of doubt and hesitation and know for what end we are in the world— but how soon we relapse into the old uncertainty ! We seek God but cannot find him ; we construct arguments to demonstrate him, but these bring conviction neither to the mind nor to the heart. Yes, we are baffled men and women in a mysterious world.

We are forced to ask why this is. There are just two possible explanations of our lot ; one is that we are the victims of fate and the other that we are guilty, we have somehow brought it upon ourselves. The choice, in other words, is between destiny and responsibility as the ultimate explanation of why our life is so problematic and un-

satisfying. It is in these terms that Heim
joins issue with the attempt, associated with
his own university of Tübingen, to create
a German religion in opposition to Christianity. For Hauer and Rosenberg the Aryan
with his acceptance of destiny is a nobler
figure than the Christian with his consciousness of guilt and yearning for forgiveness.
Heim replies that the new religion is neither
more German nor nobler than the old. It
is no more German for it was not only Luther
who looked into the depths of human nature
and shuddered at what he saw ; Kant,
Schiller, and Schopenhauer are at one with
him in this. Nor is it nobler, for whereas
destiny rivets a man to his circumstances
and permits only the braggart heroism of
blustering denial, guilt summons to repentance, repentance opens the door to forgiveness, and where the angel of mercy has
entered in, a new life is possible. But the
most important difference between the two
views has still to be mentioned. If the Norns
have spun my thread, it is for me to meet
with all my manhood what comes upon me.
I must be my own support and deliverer :

c

or, if I have a god, it will be one I have
fashioned for myself. But if, on the other
hand, I am a sinner, then my only help is
in a God beyond myself. Then the urgent
question becomes, not : How can I accept
my destiny ? but : What must I do to be
saved ?

But of course we are not the judges in
this matter ; we are not called upon to decide
between two neatly balanced hypotheses.
What happens is that Jesus arrests our consciences with the disclosure of our guilt,
and all we can do is to accept the humbling
revelation to our salvation or to spurn it
to our loss. In his presence we see that
we and all mankind are guilty before God,
that the pain, the uncertainty, and the partial
character of our life in this world are so
many signs that that life is wholly other
than what God designed it to be. At the
beginning of all human things is this Fall
which has brought ruin upon us all, but for
which we are personally responsible. To
describe what this means, Heim has recourse
to a painting by Rubens. Above is the
throne of judgment, below the pit of hell,

and in between the confused, hopeless mass
of the damned. A single thrust has impelled
them on their downward road, and now,
clinging to each other, impeding each other,
they go hurtling to the abyss. So sin entered
the world by one man and death passed upon
all.

Jesus has this clear, consistent account
of what is wrong. We are all of us involved
in a gigantic rebellion against God. This
rebellion, again, is no mere affair of individual
wills which decline to obey him. There is
a single will which pits itself against God in
utter animosity and seeks in boundless pride
to dethrone him in order to usurp his place.
That will was in the first man and it is in
us. Its name is Satan. For, while in the
objective world of daily life persons are
sharply separated from each other, in that
other and inner world there are no such
barriers ; selves are beyond time and space
and are therefore one. Satan belongs to
that world ; he is the antagonist of God
and organises us in opposition to him. That,
of course, does not absolve us from responsibility. Satan works on us, as God does,

by winning our free consent to what he
suggests. He does not coerce, he tempts,
and we are to blame when we yield to his
temptation. But Heim is emphatic that the
evil in the world is not to be explained without reference to some superhuman will. There
is about evil a subtlety, an organising ability,
a nice adjustment of means to ends, which
are not to be accounted for otherwise. We
have the impression, too, at times that vast
forces of evil are in the background, waiting
for some trivial action to bring them into
play, as when we flare up in anger at a
slight which really amounts to nothing, or
a nation goes to war in a quarrel which
could easily have been settled by arbitration.
The world is a battle ground on which two
wills contend, the good will of God and the
evil will of Satan.

Is not this to surrender to dualism, it
will be asked? No, for this opposition between Satan and God is only one side of
the truth. The other side was expressed
by Luther with characteristic boldness when
he declared that the devil was ' God's devil '
and can only work as God permits. We

cannot for one moment accept the suggestion that God is not ruler of the universe, that there is an independent power capable of frustrating his purposes. God is over all, he works all in all : without that confidence how could we pray? And yet, when we look at Gethsemane, we see that the issue of it hangs in the balance. There is a dark power which is bent on dethroning God, and it is not certain that he will be over-come—we must go as far as that. Yet, that God is on the throne and makes even the wrath of man to praise him—this also we must affirm. Faith lies in the tension be-tween these two, between the judgment of conscience that evil is against God and must be fought with all our might and the con-viction of faith that God's enemies serve his purpose unconsciously as his friends do con-sciously.

This may all be stated in terms of daily duty. The world is at once the sphere of our appointed duty, a gift to be received from the hands of God, and a battleground on which we are stationed to maintain the struggle against his adversary. The creation is good, and evil enters only by our misuse of it. He who is in a right relation to God has no need to wish that circumstances were other than they are: he is not dismayed by the contradictions of life in time and space, its baffling relativities and its painful limitations, for he sees in all this the means by which God in his goodness communicates with his children. But outside this relation to God, the world is chaos and disorder. Faith lives therefore in the tension between acceptance of the world as from God and valiant warfare against the evil which is so deeply entrenched in it. We may speak, indeed, of a right relation to God, but to that we never attain here below; we are involved in the universal rebellion of the creature against the Creator. We must live therefore by God's mercy in the forgiveness of sins and in the hope of Christ's return, which will resolve our doubts and free us from our present restraints. For the Christian is one who looks forward to a consummation yet to come.

5

CONSUMMATION

S UCH expectation means, of course, that while the question of guilt and for-giveness is the most urgent question of our life, it is not the only one. There are other concerns, those of happiness and culture, for example. Modern psychology, at least the school of Adler, would have us believe that one of the most potent of human impulses is the will to power. In recent times we have become obsessed with problems of a political and economic order, so that the whole realm of the inner life threatens to become like a foreign land to us : we have information that others have been there, but we have no knowledge of it for ourselves. Hence the New Testament becomes strange to us and we wonder whether Martin Luther was not the victim of some strong delusion. Is there any reality behind a tormented conscience? Is it perhaps only some form of psychological self-mortification? The challenge is not one to be evaded, but the modern mind needs to be told quite clearly that Jesus does not conform to its demands. He is no Aryan hero, but the Saviour of mankind from guilt and sin.

The New Testament takes us out of the common-sense world in which we spend our lives into the dynamic world which lies behind it, a world of tense drama and conflict of wills. Jesus shows us all life as the battleground on which God and Satan join issue. He speaks of his mission as one of opposition to Satan : his career begins with an encounter with him—the Temptation—and at his arrest he acknowledges that the powers of darkness have this one hour, at least, for their own. He dies that he may destroy the works of the devil. Heim follows the writer to the Hebrews by making Gethsemane the scene of this world-shaking and world-redeeming encounter. It is like a contest in a court of law, where now one party gains the upper hand and now the other, till the last tribunal decides the case beyond appeal. So Jesus allows Satan to obtain the advantage at first ; he submits without resistance and cloaks his divine power under weakness and shame. But in the end he wins the day because he is sinless and therefore, as he himself expresses it, the prince of this world has nothing in him.

The final verdict from the last tribunal is the event we speak of as the Resurrection. This belongs to the historical order and the material world, but also to spiritual reality. The body of Jesus was reanimated. That was necessary, because the victory of God must be won in this actual world, not in some realm of ideas and abstract truths. The Resurrection brings with it the enthronement of Jesus : he who was powerless upon the Cross enters thereby upon his reign. In dealing with the question of guilt, Jesus has also solved the problem of power. Indeed, the two are inseparable, for in the last resort all power belongs to God and we possess it only in so far as we are at one with him. If we fall away from him, we have only the semblance of power and not its reality. Already in his ministry, by his

healings and especially by his exorcisms,
Jesus acted as one who, just because of his
unity with the Father in mind and heart
and will, could work in the world with his
power ; and it is noticeable that he himself
regarded his healings as victories won in
conflict with demonic forces of a personal
character.

But here a problem rises. Jesus, we may
say, is *de jure* King, but not *de facto* so. At
least, that is the Protestant contention, for
we cannot accept the Catholic claim that
Christ actually rules among us in the person
of the Pope and through the hierarchy and
sacraments of the Church. Rather do we
live as those who hope for his coming again.
But, we are forced to ask, why, after the over-
throw of Satan, does not Jesus take to himself his power and reign ? Why are we his
servants left to suffer and wait ? In other
ages, it might reasonably have been suggested
that the witness of the martyrs wins souls
for their Lord, and that this is the justi-
fication for a time of waiting and trial. But
the powers of evil are more clever and subtle
in our day. The man who is spirited away

into a concentration camp in the middle of the night and is never heard of again, has no chance of making any impression upon his fellows. We live, therefore, between the times, in the interval before the last act of the world-drama. God holds back from the exercise of his power and leaves the world to its own devices till the Lord returns.

But we can see to some extent why the divine strategy is such, why it allows the enemy time to consolidate his position before launching the final attack upon him. It does so to correct the natural human desire to give the problem of power precedence over that of guilt. God must teach us that nothing matters in comparison with peace of conscience and reconciliation with him. We are so full of our schemes and projects, our plans for the future greatness of our nation or our own happiness, that we forget that we are sinners and must find pardon. Those who learn this lesson under the gracious divine discipline come together as the Church, the society of those who, having received the forgiveness of sins, now wait for the Lord's return, not in anxiety but in confidence.

They know that he has already ascended his throne and they are willing to be patient till he is revealed in power.

What is the Church? It is not a mere collection of individual disciples. It is the form under which Jesus continues his life in the world. We must make up our minds whether Jesus belongs only to the past or is still alive. If the former, then his teaching is a closed body of ideas and we have every right to raise the question how far these are valid for us who live under quite different conditions. If the latter, then Christ is a source of inspiration and guidance in the present and we live by contact with him from moment to moment. We are included within him as the passengers on a ship are included within the vessel ; we pass through the world as members of the body which is Christ. For, as we have seen, while in the static world of spatio-temporal experience selves are exclusive, they may not be so in that dynamic world which lies behind it.

We do not choose Christ, he chooses us. As he came to his first disciples by the lake, so he comes to us. ' Follow me ! ' he calls, and we leave all to follow him. We are content to take our orders from him, as the soldier does from his officer. We play our part as is required of us and leave to him the direction of the campaign as a whole. And we may well be proud to be under his banner. Earth has many heroes and many leaders, but who among them can compare with this man who won the supreme victory by accepting the most shameful defeat? 'The highest honour which can be conferred on a man is to be worthy of him, to be counted worthy to bear his cross after him and under his leadership to lay down one's life in history's decisive battle.'*

* *Jesus der Weltvollender*, 253.

FOR FURTHER READING

The New Divine Order, 1930.

The Church of Christ and the Problems of the Day, 1935.

Spirit and Truth, 1935.

God Transcendent, 1935.

The Living Fountain, 1936.

The Power of God, 1937.

Responsibility and Destiny (in *Germany's New Religion*, 1932).